SOME IMPORTANT PLACES IN LUDWIG VAN BEETHOVEN'S LIFE

1. **Bonn, Germany.** Ludwig van Beethoven was born here in 1770. Ludwig's father was a singer and musician in Bonn's royal court. He began teaching Ludwig to play keyboard instruments and the violin at an early age. Bonn, one of Germany's oldest cities, was founded over 2,000 years ago!

2. **Cologne, Germany.** Seven-year-old Ludwig gave his first public performance in the nearby city of Cologne.

3. **Vienna, Austria.** During Beethoven's time, Vienna was the center of the powerful Austrian Empire.

It was also the most important music city in Europe. Ludwig traveled to Vienna as a young man for a short visit. He later returned to spend most of his life in and around Vienna.

4. Beethoven traveled to many towns and cities where he gave piano concerts and wrote music. Some of these included **Prague**, in what is today the **Czech Republic**, and…

5. **Dresden**, **Leipzig**, and **Berlin** in Germany.

THIS IS THE AREA THAT'S SHOWN ON THE LARGER MAP

MAP OF THE ENTIRE TOTAL COMPLETE WORLD

TIMELINE OF LUDWIG VAN BEETHOVEN'S LIFE

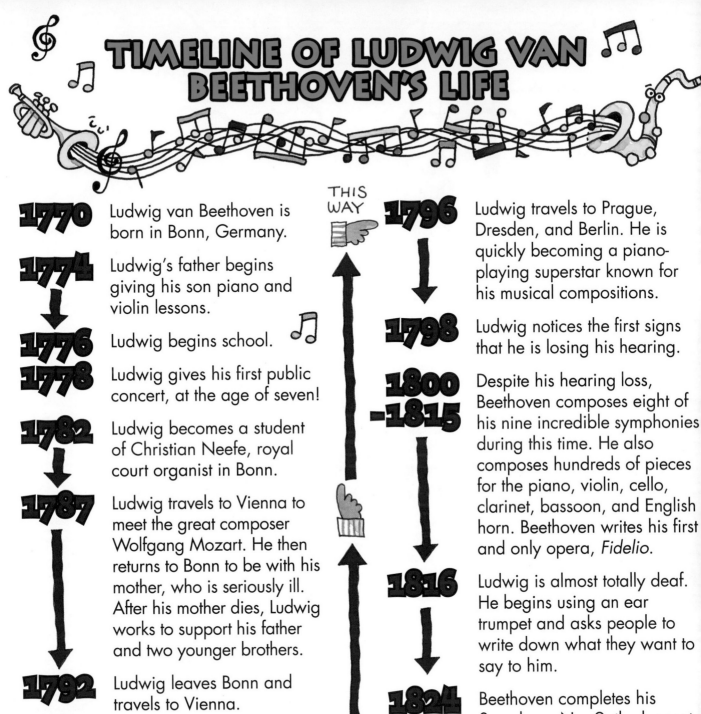

1770 Ludwig van Beethoven is born in Bonn, Germany.

1774 Ludwig's father begins giving his son piano and violin lessons.

1776 Ludwig begins school.

1778 Ludwig gives his first public concert, at the age of seven!

1782 Ludwig becomes a student of Christian Neefe, royal court organist in Bonn.

1787 Ludwig travels to Vienna to meet the great composer Wolfgang Mozart. He then returns to Bonn to be with his mother, who is seriously ill. After his mother dies, Ludwig works to support his father and two younger brothers.

1792 Ludwig leaves Bonn and travels to Vienna.

1793 In Vienna, Beethoven studies music with world-famous composer Joseph Haydn.

1795 Beethoven performs his first piano concert in Vienna.

THIS WAY

1796 Ludwig travels to Prague, Dresden, and Berlin. He is quickly becoming a piano-playing superstar known for his musical compositions.

1798 Ludwig notices the first signs that he is losing his hearing.

1800-1815 Despite his hearing loss, Beethoven composes eight of his nine incredible symphonies during this time. He also composes hundreds of pieces for the piano, violin, cello, clarinet, bassoon, and English horn. Beethoven writes his first and only opera, *Fidelio*.

1816 Ludwig is almost totally deaf. He begins using an ear trumpet and asks people to write down what they want to say to him.

1824 Beethoven completes his Symphony No. 9, the longest of his symphonies. It includes a chorus and takes over an hour to perform.

1827 Ludwig van Beethoven dies at the age of fifty-six.

UP HERE

GETTING TO KNOW
THE WORLD'S
GREATEST COMPOSERS

LUDWIG
VAN
BEETHOVEN

WRITTEN AND ILLUSTRATED BY MIKE VENEZIA

CONSULTANT
DONALD FREUND, PROFESSOR OF COMPOSITION,
INDIANA UNIVERSITY SCHOOL OF MUSIC

CHILDREN'S PRESS®

An Imprint of Scholastic Inc.

For Mike and Laura with love.

Photos ©: cover and title page: Stock Montage; 3, 6: Erich Lessing/Art Resource, NY; 8-9: RMN-Grand Palais/Art Resource, NY; 14: Bettmann/Getty Images; 15: A View of Vienna from the Belvedere, by Bernardo Bellotto/KHM-Museumsverband; 18, 19: Bettmann/Getty Images; 22 top: Beethoven-Haus Bonn, Sammlung H.C. Bodmer; 22 bottom: Beethoven-Haus Bonn; 23 top: Johann Peter Lyser/akg-images; 23 bottom: German Information Center, New York; 24: Courtesy of Steinway & Sons; 26: ClassicStock/Charles Phelps Cushing/akg-images; 28-29: Scala/Art Resource, NY; 33, 34 background: Stock Montage.

Library of Congress Cataloging-in-Publication Data

Names: Venezia, Mike, author, illustrator.
Title: Ludwig van Beethoven / written and illustrated by Mike Venezia.
Description: Revised edition. | New York : Children's Press, 2017. | Series:
  Getting to know the world's greatest composers | Includes index.
Identifiers: LCCN 2016045941| ISBN 9780531220597 (library binding) | ISBN
  9780531222416 (pbk.)
Subjects: LCSH: Beethoven, Ludwig van, 1770-1827—Juvenile literature. |
  Composers—Austria—Biography—Juvenile literature.
Classification: LCC ML3930.B4 V46 2017 | DDC 780.92 [B] —dc23 LC record available at
https://lccn.loc.gov/2016045941

SCHOLASTIC, CHILDREN'S PRESS, and associated logos are trademarks and/or registered trademarks of Scholastic Inc.
Scholastic Inc., 557 Broadway, New York, NY 10012.

6 7 8 9 10 R 26 25 24 23

A portrait of Ludwig van Beethoven

Ludwig van Beethoven was born in Bonn, Germany, in 1770. He came up with new, thrilling, and expressive ways of putting musical sounds together that changed the history of music forever.

Ludwig van Beethoven's best-known pieces were very different from the light, cheerful, classical music people were used to hearing at a royal gathering, dance, or party. Ludwig's music let people feel things about the joy, sadness, and stress of life.

It was sometimes very loud and exciting, and often beautiful enough to give you goosebumps all over—so it wasn't the kind of music that was going to go over very well at a polite party or dance.

In the early
1800s, European
musicians, writers,
and painters
wanted to express
the beauty and
wildness of nature.
This painting, by
Austrian artist
Joseph Koch,
shows a waterfall
in Switzerland.

Beethoven grew up during a time
in history when things were beginning
to change all over Europe. This period
was known as the Age of Enlightenment.
For the first time in hundreds of years,
writers, artists, and everyday people
had new respect for education, science,
new ideas, honesty, and the beauty and

wildness of nature. Also, important thinkers were saying that every person should be thought of as being equally important, even if they weren't born into a wealthy or royal family. When Beethoven was a teenager, he heard that the citizens of France started a revolution against their king and queen. They decided they were tired of being very poor and treated like servants.

Beethoven thought the people of France and their leader, Napoleon, were great heroes, fighting for the freedom and rights of everyone. A few years later, Beethoven wrote music that went along perfectly with the changing times. One of his greatest compositions, the Third Symphony, is also known as the *Eroica* ("heroic") symphony. It is filled with powerful, heroic sounds and feelings. Beethoven wrote it in honor of his favorite hero, Napoleon.

A scene from the French Revolution

When Ludwig van Beethoven was born, both his father and grandfather were singers and musicians in the court of the prince of Bonn, Germany. Mr. Beethoven could tell right away that his son had a lot of musical talent. When Ludwig was only four years old, his father started teaching him to play the piano. Ludwig was so little that he had to stand on a stool to reach the keys.

Unfortunately, Mr. Beethoven wasn't a very good father or teacher. He often drank too much alcohol and worked Ludwig very hard—hard enough to be

considered cruel by some people. It seemed like Mr. Beethoven didn't care as much about his son's future as he did about making himself famous by trying to become the father of a great musician.

By the time he was eight years old, Ludwig had become a pretty good piano player. His father invited people to their home and charged them money to hear his son play. Ludwig did only a few public performances, though. Mr. Beethoven really didn't know how to teach his son properly, and Ludwig may not have been good enough yet to have people pay to hear him.

Luckily, right around this time, the prince of Bonn hired a new court organ player. Christian Neefe was an excellent musician. He heard Ludwig play, and knew he could be a great musician someday.

Christian Neefe began teaching Beethoven in a kinder, more caring way. Ludwig kept getting better and better. When Ludwig was only twelve, Christian felt comfortable enough, every once in a while, to leave him in charge of playing the organ and directing the court orchestra all by himself!

When Beethoven was around eighteen years old, the prince of Bonn thought it might be a good idea to show him off a little bit. He was proud of Beethoven's talent, and sent Ludwig to the city of Vienna, Austria.

Music historians disagree about whether Beethoven played for Mozart—as illustrated below—or whether the two only met.

Vienna in the late 1700s

Vienna was the center of music in Europe at the time. Beethoven impressed people there, and some historians think he got a chance to play for Vienna's most famous composer, Wolfgang Amadeus Mozart. Ludwig hoped he might be able to study with the great composer, but Ludwig's mother had become seriously ill, and he returned home to be with her.

Soon after Ludwig got back to Bonn, his mother died. Not long after that, Beethoven's baby sister died. To make things worse, Ludwig's father began to drink even more, and wasn't able to work any longer as a court musician. Ludwig was worried about his father and his two younger brothers, Casper and Nikolaus. He asked the prince of Bonn if he could take over as head of the Beethoven family. The prince, who knew all about Ludwig's father,

agreed. Ludwig was relieved, but found
that running a house, caring for two
younger brothers, and trying to keep his
father out of trouble interfered a lot with
his music studies.

Even though the city of Bonn was an excellent place to learn about music, Ludwig van Beethoven really wanted to return to Vienna. Wolfgang Mozart had died by this time, but Ludwig was offered a chance to study with another one of the city's famous composers, Joseph Haydn.

Haydn read a musical piece written by Beethoven and arranged for him to be one of his students.

Joseph Haydn

Haydn leading a quartet in rehearsal

Ludwig gave his father enough money to take care of Casper and Nikolaus, and left for Vienna in 1792.

Only seven weeks later, Beethoven's father died. Beethoven's two brothers eventually joined him in Vienna, and he never returned to Bonn.

When he first arrived in his new city, Ludwig learned all about classical music from Joseph Haydn and other excellent teachers. He started to compose more music and gave concerts to make money. Ludwig van Beethoven was a big hit in Vienna, not so much for his compositions at the time, but for his great piano playing. People loved to hear his imaginative playing and watch his powerful hands move quickly across the keyboard.

He gave new twists to music, and became
as popular as any rock star is today!

Beethoven had many musical successes throughout his life. Wealthy people paid him lots of money to write his wonderful music. They were amazed by how he kept coming up with new and imaginative compositions.

But Ludwig van Beethoven also had a lot of problems. First of all, he was always deeply troubled by the way his father had brought him up. In fact, some people think that the storminess between them can be heard in Beethoven's music. Secondly, he could never seem to find the right girlfriend.

Among the women who Beethoven loved, but never married, were Giulietta Guicciardi (above) and Marie-Therese von Brunswick (left).

As many times as he fell in love, things never worked out, and he never got married.

Ludwig also had some problems with his brothers and their families. The worst thing, though, was that Beethoven began to lose his hearing just when he was starting to do his greatest work!

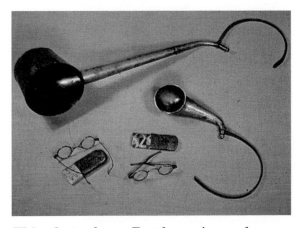

This photo shows Beethoven's eyeglasses, as well as the metal ear trumpets he used to help him hear better.

Because Beethoven had so many problems and a forceful personality, people often thought he was crabby and unfriendly. He once wrote a letter to his brothers explaining that he wasn't really a grouch. He said he sometimes ignored people because he couldn't hear them very well.

Beethoven didn't want anyone to know
that someone who was supposed to be a great
composer could hardly hear his own music!

Beethoven composing

Ludwig van Beethoven tried very hard not to let his problems get in the way of his work. He often had to struggle to write his beautiful string quartets, sonatas, concertos, and symphonies.

Beethoven is probably best known for his nine symphonies. A symphony is an important musical work played by an orchestra.

It usually has four parts, or movements. Beethoven's symphonies were more exciting than most of those that had been written before. He used bigger orchestras and sometimes had them play parts very loudly and then very softly to get different and interesting moods.

He often used a musical theme or tune over and over, changing or disguising it, or just playing a part of it, to keep his audience guessing as to what he might do next. One of Beethoven's most famous themes is only four notes long. Those four notes may be the most exciting ever written, and you can hear them in the beginning of his Fifth Symphony.

Ludwig van Beethoven always loved nature, and spent much of his time in the peaceful countryside near his home. While he could still hear, Beethoven wrote down ideas for his music from the different sounds of the forest.

In his Sixth Symphony, also known as the *Pastoral*, Beethoven created a kind of

A painting by 19th-century German Romantic painter Caspar David Friedrich

musical story, or picture, for people to imagine while they listened to it. He gave the symphony five parts instead of the usual four, and gave each one a title that described it.

The first movement is about the happy feeling you get when you arrive in the country. Then, there's a scene by a brook. The third part is the gathering of villagers. Next is the thunderstorm, and, finally, a song by a shepherd who is grateful that the storm is over.

The amazing thing about the *Pastoral* symphony is that the music is so powerful, you almost feel like you're actually in

the middle of a beautiful countryside, meadow, or forest—not just picturing it. In one section, Beethoven included actual bird songs he copied from the nightingales, quails, and cuckoos he heard while gathering his ideas.

Many people think that the music Beethoven wrote in his later years was his best. He seemed to have brought all his imagination, love, and power to these pieces. In his last symphony, the Ninth, Beethoven even added a chorus of singers to go along with the orchestra. Of all of Beethoven's music, this exciting symphony may do the best job of giving you goosebumps all over.

Ludwig van Beethoven lived to be 56 years old. In many of his joyous musical pieces he seemed to be saying, "Even with lots of problems, if you try hard enough, you can do anything you want, like I did."

It's easy find Beethoven's music. You can go online and stream his music for free. Even aliens can listen to Beethoven's music, if they're lucky enough to find *Voyager 2*. When this space probe was launched in 1977, a recording of the Fifth Symphony was included as a sample of what human beings are all about.

LEARN MORE BY TAKING THE BEETHOVEN QUIZ!

(ANSWERS ON THE NEXT PAGE.)

1. When Ludwig van Beethoven was only seven years old, he played difficult piano pieces in front of a large audience. Even so, his father was disappointed. Why?

a He was upset because he missed Ludwig's performance when he became stuck in the snack line outside the concert hall.

b Even though Ludwig did a good job, the audience gave him only a mild response.

c Little Ludwig refused to finish the concert until he got a fresh lollipop.

2. **TRUE or FALSE:** Ludwig was a brilliant student in grade school. He always brought home As and Bs on his report card.

3. **TRUE or FALSE:** Beethoven often damaged pianos while practicing his high-powered musical pieces.

4. **TRUE or FALSE:** Ludwig sometimes removed the legs of his pianos and played piano while sitting on the floor.

5. Beethoven moved quite often during the thirty-five years he lived in Vienna. How many times did he switch residences?

a 15

b 350

c Over 60

6. **TRUE or FALSE:** Beethoven was the first composer to use a large group of singers in a symphony.

ANSWERS

1. **b** Only ten years before Beethoven's first concert, little Wolfgang Mozart thrilled audiences with his brilliant playing and super-cute personality. People had gotten used to the idea that Wolfgang was the top kid star. Also, Ludwig was very serious, an attitude that audiences didn't appreciate. Mr. Beethoven was disappointed his young son was no Mozart.

2. **FALSE** Ludwig had sloppy handwriting, did poorly in math, couldn't spell very well, and didn't make friends easily. He couldn't wait to get home and practice the violin and harpsichord.

3. **TRUE** During Beethoven's time, pianos weren't as sturdy as they are today. Beethoven was always looking for a piano manufacturer that could build a piano that wouldn't fall apart during his exciting and forceful playing.

4. **TRUE** When Ludwig lost his hearing, he would sometimes take the legs off his piano. He would then sit on the floor while practicing in order to "feel" his music vibrating around and through the floorboards.

5. **c** Ludwig van Beethoven was as fussy about his living quarters as he was about his music. During the time he lived in Vienna, a restless Beethoven switched his residences at least sixty times!

6. **TRUE** Beethoven was the first great composer to use a large group of singers, called a chorus, in a symphony. In 1824, the chorus in the fourth movement of Symphony No. 9 caused the audience to explode in applause, and it still blows audiences away today!